The
National
Standardized
M⬤M
TesT

The National Standardized

MM

TesT

The Definitive Exam that Proves
Just How Good a Mom You Really Are

by Annie Pigeon

Adams Media Corporation
Holbrook, Massachusetts

Published by
Adams Media Corporation
260 Center Street, Holbrook, MA 02343

ISBN: 1-55850-837-6

Printed in Canada.

J I H G F E D C B A

Library of Congress Cataloging-in-Publication Data
Pigeon, Annie.
The National Standardized Mom Test (NSMT) : the definitive exam that will
prove just what a good mom you really are / by Annie Pigeon.
        p.   cm.
        ISBN 1-55850-837-6
1. Mothers–Humor. 2. Motherhood–Humor. I. Title.
PN6231.M68P54   1998
818'.5402–dc21   97-49435
                                    CIP

Disclaimer: Any trademarks are the property of the company that owns them,
and we make no claims to ownership or to having originated them.

Annie Pigeon can be reached at http://www.apigeon.com
Illustrations by Gary Uhl

This book is available at quantity discounts for bulk purchases.
For information, call 1-800-872-5627
(in Massachusetts, 781-767-8100).

Visit our home page at http://www.adamsmedia.com

To the parents and kids of
Fair Haven, New Jersey—
NSMT headquarters.

INSTRUCTIONS

Please read the following before beginning your test. Do not proceed to answer any questions until so instructed.

Life is a series of tests. Sometimes we know the answer instantly; sometimes we take a leap of faith; sometimes we take a wild guess.

When we were younger, tests were more predictable. We were told to eat a good breakfast and show up with two number 2 pencils. We were expected to know the difference between synonyms and antonyms, rectangles and trapezoids. We knew how to figure the length of a hypotenuse, and we remembered the value of *pi*.

Then we became mothers. And we discovered that our pre-mothering brains were to our post-mothering brains as eggs are to omelets. Everything's still in there all right, but it's a tad scrambled. For example, if anyone asked us what *pi* was today, we'd know right off the bat it was something Martha Stewart makes better than we do.

But, no matter. Life's little exams are different now. Our children test us daily, and we rise to the occasion. So what if our "good breakfast" consists of a pop-up toaster snack and our number 2 pencils have been replaced with stubby Crayolas? As Moms, we possess a wealth of wisdom unequaled by history's greatest sages.

We are steeped in the lore of practical, hands-on child-rearing with knowledge of everything from infant lullabies to teenage alibis. We know the school holiday calendar by heart. We know exactly who will tolerate what in their lunchbox. We know just when Gap Kids will have its rock-bottom clearance sale. We can tell you how to mix and match a great Barbie ensemble. And, heaven help us, we can actually name most of Thomas the Tank Engine's friends.

Until now, we couldn't actually prove just how savvy we were. But now, thanks to the National Standardized Mom Test (NSMT), we'll have a chance to amaze our loved ones with evidence of our expertise.

The NSMT is modeled on actual standardized tests and consists of multiple choice, true–false, reading comprehension, vocabulary, logic, and mathematics questions—one hundred in total—all relating to the challenging world of contemporary motherhood.

How much time do I have to take the test?

The same amount of time you have for everything else that seems like lots of fun, i.e., virtually no time at all. However, you may take this test in start-and-stop fashion, in those stolen moments when the kids are napping, or off at school, or engaged in a quiet play activity such as painting a wall mural with spaghetti sauce.

What if I don't have a pop-up toaster snack and some stubby Crayolas?

No problem. We accept pre-test breakfasts of Froot Loops, string cheese, or even a simple shot of grape juice. And your test responses may be written with magic markers, sidewalk chalk, or mashed peas.

Is this some sort of joke or something?

You see, you *are* a smart cookie, after all. This *is* some sort of joke. Or something. We expect you to take the NSMT with your tongue lodged firmly in your cheek.

You may now turn to the first page of the test and begin.

PART ONE

MULTIPLE CHOICE

20 QUESTIONS
Select the best answer from among
the choices provided. Sometimes
more than one answer is correct.

1. **As a mother, which phrase comes in most handy?**

A. We'll see . . .
B. Because I'm your mother, that's why.
C. We can't afford it.
D. I *told* you to be careful with that.
E. Ahhhhhhhh!

The correct answer is E.

2. What are the four food groups?

A. Grains/dairy/meats and fish/fruits and vegetables.
B. Sweets/nitrates/sugar-laden high-sodium breakfast cereals/coins, paper clips, and other small metal objects which may require the use of the Heimlich maneuver.
C. Food they like/foods they hate/foods they throw/foods they throw up.

B and C are equally correct answers. If you answered A, wake up and smell the soda pop.

3. When will your children get up from their nap?

A. After they've had a full, refreshing sleep cycle that will improve their mood and provide energy for cooperative play.
B. When a pin drops three houses away.
C. Before your flavored, instant international coffee has cooled enough for you to take even one sip.

The answer is A—in your dreams, ha ha!

4. What is the best thing about breastfeeding?

A. Your babies will receive the benefit of your immunities and antibodies, making them healthier than bottle-fed babies.

B. Your infants will bond with you deeply, making them more emotionally secure than bottle-fed babies.

C. You get to feel superior toward mothers who use formula.

D. Cleavage.

A and B have never been definitively proven.
Both C and D are correct answers.

5. How can you tell when you are sleep-deprived?

A. You have out-of-body experiences hovering over the produce aisle at the A&P.

B. You, um, can't seem to find stuff once you put it down.

C. There's, uh, some other way you can tell, but it slips your mind.

The answer is . . . what was the question again?

6. Your babies are cutest when . . .

A. They're dressed up for Halloween in one of those little "pea-in-a-pod" costumes.
B. They're hugging a stuffed animal that's much bigger than they are.
C. They're smiling up at you adoringly and saying "Gloo ga moo ma."
D. They're asleep.
E. You're asleep.

The correct answer is D. If you answered E, see the preceding question.

7. Why have strollers become so complicated?

A. Because a secret cabal of stroller makers is successfully staging an international plot to drive Moms over the edge.

B. So your infants will simply have to stop being such "babies" and learn to sit up sooner.

C. So Dads can feel smug when they finally help you get the back of the seat down to a horizontal position.

The correct answer is C. If you answered A, don't be paranoid. No such plot is necessary, as most Moms are already over the edge.

8. What is the source of Barney's secret depression?

A. He thinks purple isn't really flattering to him.
B. He can't decide if he's a carnivore or an herbivore.
C. He fears his species will be obliterated by a giant meteorite.
D. He would have preferred to be cast in a featured role in *Jurassic Park*.

The correct answer, according to his agent, is D.

9. How many "friends" does Thomas the Tank Engine have?

A. 66
B. 666
C. Enough to max out your credit card.
D. They're not really his friends, they're just a bunch of cheesy hangers-on, and if your kids knew what was good for them, they'd spend some time playing with live children instead of those overpriced, wooden stooges.

The correct answer is C. If you answered A or B, you took the question too literally. If you answered D, hey, lighten up.

10. **The literary quote: "I will not eat them in a house. I do not like them with a mouse" is originally from:**

A. *Green Eggs and Ham.*
B. *Good Night Moon.*
C. *The Very Hungry Caterpillar.*
D. *Shakespeare's Collected Sonnets.*
E. The Bible.

The correct answer is E; however it is secretly encoded.

11. When was the last time you were actually alone in the bathroom?

A. Sometime in the 1980s.
B. The day you locked yourself in until Dad finally took the kids to the park.
C. Just before you went into labor.
D. The day you sneaked over to the Sunoco station for some peace and quiet.

The correct answer is C.

12. Which method of discipline is most effective?

A. Time-outs.
B. Cash bribes.
C. Ultimatums and threats.
D. Shameless begging and pleading.
E. Plying with ice cream.

The answer is B; however, E may work if you throw in rainbow sprinkles.

13. When asked, "What happened at school today?" your child will most likely answer . . .

A. I absorbed a meaningful lesson in multicultural diversity.
B. I decided I definitely want to be a neurosurgeon.
C. Billy made in his pants.
D. Nothing.
E. I finally got a handle on logarithms.

The correct answer is D. Score half a point for C.

14. Your nine-year-old daughter left you to babysit her Tamagotchi "baby" and it "expired." What do you tell her?

A. "Must have been, er, some defective chip or something."

B. "They don't make foreign cars like they used to, either."

C. "Thank goodness *you* weren't a computerized baby."

D. "Whoopsie-daisy!"

The correct answer is B.

15. Can't they make Play-Doh so it doesn't get all dry and crumbly?

A. No, they can't.
B. Sure they can, but then you wouldn't have to buy more Play-Doh.
C. A crack team of Nobel laureates is working on the problem even now.
D. My therapist says it's not healthy to worry too much about stuff like this.

The correct answer is C. When the Nobel laureates come up with something, we'll let you know.

16. When is the best time to start potty training?

A. When your child is two.
B. When your child is three.
C. When you have used so many disposable diapers they are about to name a landfill after you.
D. When your child no longer insists on wearing the potty on his/her head.
E. When your child complains that he's the only one on the varsity swim team in Huggies.

The correct answer is D. If you answered E, we hate to break it to you, but your baby is growing up.

17. When is the best time to move your child from a crib to a bed?

A. When your child is one and a half.
B. When your child is two and a half.
C. When you are sick and tired of those incredibly hard-to-change crib sheets.
D. When your child routinely stands in the crib.
E. When your child routinely jumps over the bars, pockets the car keys, and sneaks down to the all-night diner for a burger.

The correct answer is C. If you answered E, see previous question.

18. How will adding your teenager to your car insurance affect your policy?

A. Your rates will be lowered.

B. Your rates will stay the same.

C. Your rates will be slightly higher.

D. Your rates will make the national debt look like chump change.

E. What car insurance?

The correct answer is E.

19. As a Mom, which of these will you spend the most time searching for?

A. Missing Lego pieces.
B. Missing Brio trains.
C. The other sock.
D. Your car keys.
E. The meaning of life.

The correct answer is C.

20. Of the items listed in the previous question, which are you least likely ever to find?

A. The Legos.
B. The trains.
C. The sock.
D. The keys.
E. The meaning of life.

The correct answer is E. According to some gurus, however, you become instantly enlightened if you find all the missing socks.

10 QUESTIONS
Choose the best answer to
the questions from the
choices listed below. Sometimes
more than one choice is acceptable.

1. This baby bottle is half empty
   because . . .

A. Your baby already drank half of it, and after a nice burp will drink the rest.
B. You already spilled half on your new Ultrasuede outfit.
C. You ran out of milk.
D. The bottle isn't half empty, it's half full!

Either B or C are correct answers. If you answered A, you should get together with the people who answered D and seek reality therapy.

2. **If four years' tuition to Harvard will cost $240,000 by the time your child is eighteen, how many bags of each denomination of money will cover your child's college costs?**

Denomination A Denomination B Denomination C

A. Two C bags and two A bags.
B. Three B bags and two A bags.
C. A couple of A bags ought to do it.

The correct answer is C. Who said your child would get into Harvard?

3. Late one evening, your child jams his big toe into a door and cries out in pain. What do you do?

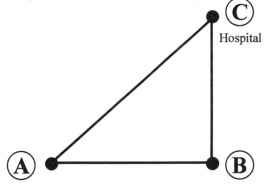

A. You proceed to the closest hospital along lines AB and BC.
B. You proceed to the closest hospital along line AC.
C. You consult your managed care brochure, find out that the only hospital in it is 136 miles due east and accepts emergencies only on Tuesdays. You then kiss the booboo, apply ice, and hope for the best.

The correct answer is C.

4. A mother of three young children plans to do two loads of laundry on Sunday, and one each on alternating days through the following Saturday. Throughout the week, what is the total number of laundry loads she does?

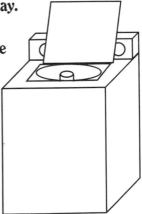

A. Six.
B. Five.
C. Seven.
D. Between twenty-two and twenty-six loads, since "planning" has nothing to do with what actually happens in her household.
E. None, because her washing machine broke down, and the repair man is still laughing hysterically at her gullibility in calling the "twenty-four-hour emergency service hotline."

Either D or E are correct answers.

5. The following pie chart represents a parental survey response to the question, "Have you ever used television as a babysitter?"

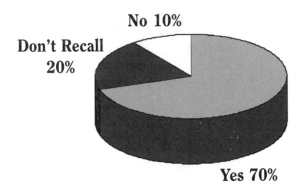

No 10%

Don't Recall 20%

Yes 70%

What conclusion can you draw from this pie chart?

A. Thirty percent of those who answered were lying.
B. Of the liars, the twenty percent who say they "don't recall" watch too much *Court TV* themselves.
C. The pie crust doesn't look flaky enough. The oven should have been more thoroughly preheated.
D. All of the above.

The correct answer is D.

6. **Tiffany has three more cream-filled cookies than Jason. Each child breaks his/her cream-filled cookies in half. The algebraic equation representing the number of cookies Jason actually eats is:**

A. $\dfrac{x-3}{2}$ C. $\dfrac{2}{3(x)}$

B. $\dfrac{x+3}{2}$ D. $\mathbf{0}$

The correct answer is D. Jason doesn't actually eat any cream-filled cookies because he is lactose intolerant. However, if you are not personally acquainted with Jason, you earn credit if you attempted to understand the question.

7. The following bar graph represents a parental survey response to the question, "Do you ever wish you'd chosen to raise goldfish instead of children?"

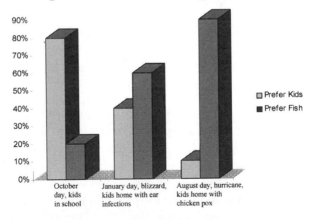

What conclusion can you draw from this graph?

A. Many people are more fond of their children when they are not actually with them.

B. Sales of goldfish go up with the incidence of both natural weather disasters and childhood illness.

C. This survey was sponsored by the National Goldfish Lobby.

D. You can't remember how to read a bar graph, but this one gets points for neatness.

The correct answer is C.

8. These two cookies were brought to the PTA bake sale by two mothers.

Cookie A

Cookie B

Cookie A is homemade, and Cookie B is store-bought. What else is the difference between the two cookies?

A. Cookie A has more chocolate chips than Cookie B.

B Cookie B has more chips than Cookie A.

C. Cookie A is larger.

D. Cookie B is larger.

E. Cookie B inflicted more guilt, and cost its buyer $440 in therapy sessions.

The correct answer is E.

9. Mrs. P has six grocery coupons.
   Three save her twenty-five cents
   each on cereal. Two save her
   twenty cents on grape juice. One
   saves her fifty cents on a box of
   crackers. If Mrs. P buys two boxes
   of cereal, one bottle of grape juice
   and two boxes of crackers, how
   much money will she save in total?

A. $1.20.
B. None, because she left her coupons at home on the kitchen counter.
C. None, because she didn't remember the coupons were in her purse until after she'd paid full price for the items.
D. None, because when she presented her coupons to the cashier, the cashier mocked her publicly and called her "coupon-challenged" because the coupons actually expired last January.

In the best of all possible worlds, the correct answer is A. Here on earth, however, the correct answers are B, C, or D.

10. Mrs. P must get Justin to soccer practice at 3:30 P.M. and to lacrosse at 4:30. She must also get Jacqueline and Corey to karate at 3:30 and swim team at 4:30.

   Mrs. Q must get Trevor and Caitlin to karate at 3:30 and Dustin to lacrosse at 4:30.

X Soccer   X Swim Team

X Lacrosse   X Karate

The following conditions apply:

- Mrs. P only has room for two in her minivan, because she has just come back with a load from Price Club.
- Dustin and Justin cannot be in the same vehicle, or they will pound each other with lacrosse sticks.
- Corey gets carsick.

What should Mrs. P and Mrs. Q do?

A. Withdraw their children from all extracurricular activities and encourage more TV watching.
B. Get Corey some Dramamine.
C. Get Dustin and Justin some handcuffs.
D. Seriously consider birth control in the future.
E. Give the kids bus fare, wish them luck, and spend the afternoon at a day spa.

D and E are correct answers.

10 QUESTIONS
Word usage: select the best answer from among the choices provided.

1. "Nyaa, nyaa," said Samantha to her sister Jennifer, "You are a poopyhead!"

   In this context, the word *poopyhead* is closest in meaning to:

   A. Weewee-brain.
   B. Stinky pants.
   C. Fat pig.
   D. Less-than-adequate playmate.
   E. Cherished sibling.

The correct answer is E, but sometimes Samantha has trouble expressing her true feelings.

2. **When her kids asked for a pony, the distracted, overtired Mom said, "Maybe."**

   In this context, the word maybe is closest in meaning to:

   A. Possibly.

   B. Perhaps.

   C. Go away and leave me alone.

   D. Get real.

   E. The meaning of the word is ambiguous and hence subject to interpretation. It clearly leaves the door open for a clever attorney to press an actual pony on this unsuspecting mother.

The correct answer, which we have verified with the American Bar Association, is E.

3. **When Mom is in the delivery room giving birth, Dad yells, "Push!"**

   In this context, the word *push* **is closest in meaning to:**

   A. Shove.
   B. Bear down.
   C. I'm gonna throw up.
   D. I don't have a clue what I'm talking about, but I paid good money for that Lamaze class.
   E. I hereby give you license to shower me with barbed insults for getting you into this condition and for simply being a male in the first place.

The correct answer is E.

4. When Mom says "Time for bed," her kids answer, "Just five more minutes!"

   In this context the phrase *five more minutes* means:

A. Thirty minutes.
B. An hour and a half.
C. We're not going anywhere until we see Letterman's Top 10 List.
D. Why don't *you* go to bed? You're the one who's always saying you're tired.

The correct answer—and, hey, not a bad idea—is D.

5. When Mom says "Share!" Tyler says, "I *am* sharing!"

In this context, when Tyler says "*I am sharing*," he means:

A. I'm politely taking turns and engaging in cooperative play.
B. I'm letting the other kids play with stuff I don't like.
C. I'm letting the other kids play with stuff I already broke.
D. I'm loaning out my toys as part of a profitable leasing program.

The correct answer, which we have verified by checking Tyler's piggy bank, is D.

6. **When Mom asks her second-grader, "Did you eat the carrot sticks I put in your lunch?" the answer is "Yeah."**

   In this context, "*Yeah*" means:

A. Yes, Mother.
B. No, ma'am.
C. I put them up my nose and pretended to be a walrus.
D. I traded them for gummy worms.
E. They're in my pocket with yesterday's broccoli florets.

The correct answer is C.

7. At 3 A.M., for the fifth time that night, the newborn baby said, "Waaaa!"
In this context, *waaaa* means:

A. I'm *hungry*.

B. I'm wet.

C. I said I'm *hungry*. Don't we have anything besides milk?

D. Wow, it would appear that simply by screaming like this I can make Mom show up—just like that. Cool! I'm gonna try it again.

The correct answer is D.

8. **When the newborn screams at 3 A.M., Dad rolls over and says, "Zzzzz–Mmmppff–Zzzzz."**
   In this context, *Zzzzz–Mmmppff–Zzzzz* means:

A. What's with that cat?
B. Oh, is that some kind of baby or something?
C. What do you want from me? I'm not the one with the mammary glands!
D. Must be my turn, honey!

The correct answer is D, but Dad often has trouble expressing his true feelings.

Analogies: choose the related words or phrases that have a relationship similar to that expressed in the original pair (e.g., black is to white as day is to night).

9. *Midnight feedings* are to *your sex life* as:

A. *Orthodonture* is to *your bank account.*
B. *Tantrums* are to *your nervous system.*
C. *Car sickness* is to *your vacation.*
D. *Spit up* is to *your wardrobe.*
E. All of the above.

The correct answer is E.

10. *Socks and underwear* are to *good Christmas gifts* as:

A. *A weed whacker* is to *a good Father's Day present.*
B. *A new protractor* is to *a neat graduation choice.*
C. *An oboe plus a* Teach Yourself Oboe book is to *a cool birthday gift.*
D. *A new vacuum* is to *a great Mother's Day selection.*

The correct answer is D. So if you gave socks and underwear last Christmas, don't look now, but here comes your new Hoover.

PART TWO

MULTIPLE CHOICE

20 QUESTIONS
Select the best answer from among the choices provided. Sometimes more than one answer is correct.

1. How do you know you're really in hard labor?

A. Contractions are ten minutes apart.
B. Contractions are two to five minutes apart.
C. You've already run through all the vile names you can think of to call your husband and start repeating yourself.
D. You genuinely couldn't care less how your hair looks.

The correct answer is D.

2. How can you tell when your "baby-proofing" has gone too far?

A. A small explosive device is needed to access the cabinet under the kitchen sink.

B. A SWAT team could not gain entry into your toolshed.

C. You have so many rubber-coated surfaces you cannot tell the difference between your living room and a Rubbermaid factory.

D. You can't remember the combination that will let you get at the cooking sherry.

The correct answer is D.

3. What is the greatest advantage of having a baby monitor?

A. It enables you to stay up all night obsessively listening to your child's breathing.

B. It enables you to stay up all night eavesdropping on the neighbors.

C. It enables you to fall into a broken sleep, dreaming that the static you hear is actually the sound of aliens abducting your child aboard their spacecraft.

D. It enables you to keep the economy growing by buying a new one every three months when the old one breaks.

The correct answer is B.

4. What does Barbie have that you don't?

A. A dream house.
B. A sports car.
C. A drop-dead wardrobe.
D. Gravity-defying breasts.
E. All of the above.

The correct answer is . . . too depressing to think about.

5. What do you have that Barbie doesn't?

A. Stretch marks.
B. Eye bags.
C. A one-minute bladder.
D. Children.
E. All of the above.

The correct answer is . . . ditto.

6. Which is the scariest movie for young children?

A. *The Lost World.*
B. *Halloween III.*
C. *Bambi.*
D. The video of that birthday party where your child threw up all over Great-Aunt Naomi.

The answer—ask any preschooler—is C.

7. How much should you spend on a child's birthday party?

A. $50.
B. $150.
C. $300.
D. More than your neighbors spent.
E. It doesn't matter, as long as your children know you love them.

The correct answer is D.

Then the correct answer is E.

8. What if the neighbors spent $2,800?

$2,800?

69

9. Why do juice boxes always spray juice when you put that little straw in?

A. Because the juice box manufacturers are secretly in cahoots with the stain remover manufacturers.

B. Because juice in the face is good for your complexion.

C. No one else's juice boxes do that— you must be doing something wrong.

The correct answer, according to the National Juice Box Council, is C.

10. Why is everyone driving a minivan?

A. Because they ran out of armored tanks.
B. Because the soccer team complained when you tried to squeeze them into a Miata.
C. Because everyone else is driving one.
D. Since strollers have become so complex, walking is no longer an option

The correct answer is A.

11. Why do they call them "minivans" anyway?

A. Because the term "gas-guzzling, impossible-to-park road hog" did not test well with focus groups.

B. Because Disney had already patented "Mickey van."

C. Because "maxivan" sounded like a feminine hygiene product.

D. Because who has time to argue?

The correct answer is D.

12. What is the best thing about taking a trans-Atlantic flight with your three-month-old?

A. It builds character to be the object of universal scorn.
B. You always hated flight attendants anyhow.
C. After giving birth, getting thrown up on at 30,000 feet is a cakewalk.
D. It is several hours shorter than a trans-Pacific flight.

The correct answer is B.

13. What is the greatest invention in the history of humankind?

A. Velcro.

B. Sippy cups.

C. The wheel.

D. Washable markers.

E. That gizmo you pop on the front of your VCR to keep your toddlers from wrecking it.

The correct answer would be D, if washable markers were actually washable. Since they are not, we'll go with E.

14. What is a good response when your child threatens to run away from home?

A. Fine. I'll pack you some Cheerios.
B. Fine. Don't forget your blankie.
C. Fine. Don't forget your cell phone— and fax us if you land a high-paying position.
D. Oh, please don't go. You can watch *Freakazoid* during dinner and keep the snake in the tub and *everything*.
E. Fine.

E will suffice. If you answered D, have a little dignity, will you?

15. Why doesn't everyone else realize your kid's a genius?

A. Not everyone sees the timeless beauty in rice cereal sculptures.

B. Some people are just too dense to realize your babbling toddler is quoting James Joyce.

C. Auto industry spies stole the crayon drawing that explicitly outlines plans for a car that runs on used wet wipes.

D. They do realize; they just won't admit it because they're jealous.

The correct answer is D.

16. Just what is it that Mr. Rogers is high on?

A. Helium from party balloons.
B. Wool fibers from cardigan sweaters.
C. The Nielson ratings.
D. Life.

The correct answer, or so his publicist would have us believe, is D.

17. If Martha Stewart came to your house, what would you give her?

A. Fresh-ground coffee and homemade *petit fours*.
B. A festive brunch complete with hand-embroidered napkins.
C. A nine-course gourmet banquet.
D. Reheated Chinese takeout.
E. A heart attack.

The correct answer is D, to be followed shortly by E.

18. Given access to a push-button phone, your average one-year-old will . . .

A. Dial Greenland.
B. Report you to the authorities.
C. Arrange to change your long distance carrier.
D. Try to eat the receiver.

The correct answer, according to phone company records, is A.

19. When you are not at home, your children will . . .

A. Drink straight from the carton.
B. Go "exploring" in your dresser drawers.
C. Watch forbidden television shows.
D. Get out the vacuum and straighten up.

The correct answer is D, but it's hard to vacuum up all that shattered crystal.

20. Life is too short to . . .

A. Separate lights from darks.
B. Iron sheets, towels, or underwear.
C. Make soups, sauces, or baked goods from scratch.
D. Answer this question!

Correct answers are A, B, and C. If you answered D—very funny.

READING COMPREHENSION

10 QUESTIONS

Attempt to decipher this note from the babysitter and answer the related questions. (*In this section, correct answers are grouped at the end of each passage's questions.*)

Hi!

Amanda and Ricky are at the neighbors. I had to leave early because I forgot tonight was ~~Melrose Pla~~ math team meeting. Also, Puffy ran out— even though you said she was a house cat. I think she got scared by the swords and stuff. Don't worry about the bloodstains on the rug. My mom says they come right out with Spic and Shout.

CASEY

1. Do you think Casey really went to a math team meeting?

A. Yes
B. No
C. The text would seem to indicate there is some doubt in the matter.
D. Yeah, sure, and Heather Locklear is a Rhodes scholar.

2. What do you think the sitter meant by "swords and stuff?"

A. Swords and the good kitchen knives.
B. Swords and the good gardening shears.
C. Surely some cute, harmless play scenario the kids were acting out.
D. Don't know, but when I find out I'm going to kill her.

3. What do you think she meant by "Spic and Shout?"

A. Spic and Span.
B. Shout spot remover.
C. Perhaps she imagines that if I speak to the rug, or possibly raise my voice to it, it will clean itself.
D. Don't know, but when I find out I'm going to kill her.

4. Where do you think Puffy got to, anyway?

A. Up a tree.
B. Merrily chasing squirrels.
C. Fooling around with that tomcat around the corner.
D. Sorry, I didn't pay attention to the question, due to that horrible brake screeching and "meow-splat" sound outside.

5. Which of the neighbors do you think Amanda and Ricky are at?

A. The Smiths.
B. The Browns.
C. The Petersons.
D. Don't know who Amanda and Ricky are. My children are named Jillian and Cody.

The correct answers are:

1. D
2. D
3. D
4. *Lucky for Puffy,* C
5. D

Attempt to decode this letter
from the teacher and answer
the related questions.

Dear [insert Name of Parent]:

On Thursday, June 4, our class will be taking
a field trip to the aquarium. Given the unfortunate
events during our recent trips to the zoo (we are
happy to report that Jessica and the giraffe are,
at last, off the critical list) and the botanical
garden (our lawsuit is still pending) we seriously
hope we can persuade some of you to
accompany us as chaperones.

Sure, we've heard all your paltry excuses about "making a living" or "staying home with the newborn." But I, for one, am sick and tired of you thinking you can just pawn your kids off on us and we'll keep them out of mortal danger while you get off scot free. Even the best of teachers have "off days" when we see strange auras, and hear shrill sounds, and forget our medication, and just want to SCREAM. Quite frankly, we could use a little back-up.

Anyhoo, the sign-up sheet is above the cubbies. We look forward to a wonderful day!

Ms. Jeffers

1. How might Ms. Jeffers's letter make most Moms feel?

A. Guilty.
B. Excited about the trip.
C. Mildly concerned.
D. Lightly hysterical.
E. Litigious.

2. Why do you think the whole Jessica-and-the-giraffe incident occurred?

A. No safety muzzle on giraffe.
B. No safety muzzle on Jessica.
C. Gross negligence and incompetence on the part of Ms. Jeffers.
D. Just one of those things.
E. Because Jessica's Mom selfishly insisted on giving birth to Jessica's little sister that day instead of going along on the trip.

3. What happened at the botanical gardens?

A. Not in the text.
B. Not in the text, but I hear it involved some bonsai, a Venus fly trap, and some very unhappy little boys.
C. Not in this text, but surely you read about it in *The Enquirer*.
D. Just one of those things.

4. What thought did you have when you learned Ms. Jeffers seems to be suffering unusual symptoms?

A. Perhaps she'd best be checked out by a qualified physician.
B. Perhaps she needs a sabbatical.
C. I knew we should have sprung for private school.
D. What unusual symptoms?

5. **Why do you think Ms. Jeffers used the word "anyhoo" instead of "anyhow?"**

A. She can't spell.
B. Sheesh, she was just trying to be light and breezy.
C. She can spell, but she can't type.
D. She's a real card, that Ms. Jeffers.

5. *D*
4. *D*
3. *D*
2. *E*
1. *A*

The correct answers are:

10 QUESTIONS
Answer each question True or False. (In this section, correct answers are grouped at the end.)

1. Portions of your brain exit with the placenta. _____

2. Occasionally, you sound exactly like *your* mother. _____

3. What's good for them, your kids will hate; what's bad for them, they'll crave. _____

4. Your teenagers find you embarrassing. _____

5. Your kids will be thirty
before they figure you know
anything, and forty before
they'll admit it. _____

6. Childhood zips by in the blink of
an eye. _____

7. You'll only remember
the good parts. _____

8. Your kids will only remember
the good parts. _____

9. Having your children around is
   actually not as tough as letting
   them go. _____

10. Someday you'll look back
    at it all and have a good,
    long laugh. _____

The correct answers are:

1. *True.*	6. *False.*
2. *True.*	7. *True.*
3. *True.*	8. *False.*
4. *True.*	9. *Too true.*
5. *True,*	10. *We certainly*
hope so.	

PART THREE

MULTIPLE CHOICE

20 QUESTIONS
Select the best answer from among
the choices provided. Sometimes
more than one answer is correct.

1. Why does a pregnant woman send her husband out for pickles and ice cream in the middle of the night?

A. Because she craves the salt in the pickles and the calcium in the ice cream.

B. So she can sprawl across the entire bed while he's gone.

C. Because she can.

The correct answer is C.

2. How can you tell if you're pregnant with a boy?

A. You're carrying low.
B. You're carrying high.
C. You feel an indescribable urge to collect action figures.
D. Your mother-in-law tells you so.

The correct answer is D.

3. How can you tell when your little ones are teething?

A. You no longer own any clothes without permanent drool stains on the shoulders.

B. Their mood swings make you certain they inherited the manic-depressive gene from Aunt Zelda.

C. They start preferring peanut brittle and Turkish taffy to mashed bananas.

D. Those bite marks on your arm don't mean Count Dracula's in town.

E. All of the above.

The correct answer is E.

4. When are you most irresistible to your kids?

A. When they are not feeling well and you offer your finest TLC.

B. When you are not feeling well and they get to make you breakfast in bed.

C. When you tell them those warm, fuzzy stories about when you were a little girl

D. When Dad is being a grouch.

E. When you are on a critical, long-distance phone call.

The correct answer is E.

5. Did you remember to pay capital gains tax on your kids' tooth fairy income?

A. Yes.
B. No.
C. Omigosh, I never realized . . .

*The correct answer is C. Your audit will
follow shortly.*

6. Who said, "A little fast food never killed anyone?"

A. Ronald McDonald.
B. Chuck E. Cheese.
C. You, when you couldn't deal with fixing dinner.
D. The Food and Drug Administration, but they were just kidding.
E. All of the above.

The correct answer is E.

7. **What was the best reason to give
your kids for not buying them a
"Tickle Me Elmo"?**

A. Couldn't afford the black market
price of $500.
B. What a bunch of hype.
C. I did buy a Tickle Me Elmo, but sent
it to some poor Third World children
who needed it more than we do.
D. I drove to 46 retail outlets, placed
classified ads, even surfed the Net,
but could not find one anywhere.
So sue me!

*The correct answer is D, though on second
thought you may want to leave off the "sue
me" suggestion.*

8. Why is it called "Toys Я Us"?

A. Because the toys are dyslexic.

B. Because the toys never learned proper grammar.

C. Because "Big Ugly Warehouse Full of Irritating, Overpriced Plastic" was too long.

D. It represents a deep, philosophical statement on the nature of existence—for what are we, really, but mere toys in the endless aisles of the cosmos.

E. Just to make you crazy.

The correct answer is D.

9. What is the most important thing to teach your children about money?

A. It doesn't grow on trees.
B. Save it for a rainy day.
C. A penny saved is a penny earned.
D. Don't tell Grandma we cashed in those bonds, or no TV for a month.

The correct answer is D, but don't tell Grandma.

10. When asked which TV personality they'd most wish to be like, most Moms answered . . .

A. June Cleaver.
B. Donna Reed.
C. Olivia Walton.
D. Margaret Anderson.
E. Columbo.

The correct answer is E, however, there were a number of write-in votes for Ellen DeGeneres.

11. What do you say when your child asks, "Why are there so many Santas?"

A. The real Santa lives at the North Pole; all these others are his helpers.
B. Santa's Mom took Perganol.
C. Shhh!
D. First they cloned sheep, now this!

The correct answer is C.

12. Given Santa's weight issue, what is an appropriate snack to leave for him on Christmas Eve?

A. Carrot sticks.
B. Nonfat cottage cheese.
C. Snackwells.
D. Butter-laden shortbread cookies and whole milk.

According to the American Heart Association, correct answers are A, B, or C. But, hey, which would you rather have—a correct answer, or presents?

13. Do you think Bert and Ernie are more than "just friends?"

A. Yes.
B. No.
C. None of our business.
D. I'd ask them, but they're off vacationing in Provincetown.

The correct answer is C.

14. Which of the following is a side effect of mothering?

A. Hypochondria.
B. Paranoia.
C. Attention-deficit disorder.
D. None of the above.

The correct answer is D, but we can't dwell on it, because we have to rush the kids to the pediatrician, if the pediatrician hasn't been sued for malpractice and disappeared, and if we could only remember where the pediatrician's office is . . .

15. How will you ever get your teenage daughter off the phone?

A. Have her left ear surgically removed.
B. Yell "Fire!"
C. Tell her the phone obscures the view of her nose ring.
D. You don't want to get her off the phone, because if you do you'll just have to drive her to the mall.

The correct answer is D.

16. What would be the *least* advisable thing to say to your grown son at his wedding?

A. "I keep thinking about when I changed your diapers."
B. "And we had such high hopes for you."
C. "But can she make potato pancakes?"
D. "You'll be back!"
E. "Just send us the bill."

The correct answer is E.

17. What is the best advice for teaching your own kids to drive?

A. Remain calm.
B. Buckle up.
C. Remind them you still love them despite that jack-knifed tractor trailer incident.
D. Try not to alarm them by yelling: "Omigod we're all going to die!" too frequently.
E. Don't.

The correct answer is E.

18. **When your college-aged kids do not phone you on Sunday, you may assume . . .**

A. They're studying.
B. They're in the hospital.
C. They already have plenty of spending money.
D. Why bother to call when they're on their way over to drop off their laundry?

The correct answer is D.

19. How can you tell if you are a really good mother?

A. Your children haven't sued you yet.
B. You still have money left in the college fund, even after paying for their therapy.
C. Your children routinely tell playground bullies, "My Mom can beat your Mom."
D. You'd never spend time taking a stupid quiz like this when you could be sharing quality time with your offspring instead.

The correct answer is C.

20. Of the following, who is the best mother?

A. Mother Goose.
B. Mother Nature.
C. Ma Bell.
D. You.

The correct answer, according to your children, whom we have personally polled, is D.

We know you are anxious to find out how you did on the NSMT.

To compute your MQ (Mothering Quotient), simply count up the number of questions you answered correctly. You may also add to your score any questions you thought you answered correctly, even though another supposedly "correct" answer was given. (Hey, unlike your kids, we don't want to argue with you.)

You'll be happy to know that in the opinion of the NSMT steering committee, everyone deserves credit simply for taking the test in lieu of doing something actually productive like, say, the dishes. Therefore, next to each scoring level we have listed a prize or group of prizes which we believe you should badger your family into giving you to commemorate your level of accomplishment.

Your Score	Your Prize(s)
0–20	An autographed picture of Joan Crawford
20–40	A T-shirt that says, "I took the NSMT and all I got was this stupid T-shirt."
40–60	Dinner at a restaurant that doesn't have a "fun meal"
60–80	Tickets to a movie that is not animated, not G-rated, and does not star Tim Allen
80–100	A ticker-tape parade, your own talk show, and a half-hour dialing spree to the Home Shopping Network

Lots of luck in getting your family to come up with your commemorative prizes. And lots of luck in your future endeavors.

See you at Mom U.